Bird Words

Snippets and Snapshots of Our Feathered Friends

John Yunker

Ashland Creek Press

Bird Words
Snippets and Snapshots
of Our Feathered Friends

Published by Ashland Creek Press
Ashland, Oregon
www.ashlandcreekpress.com

© 2018 John Yunker

ISBN 978-1-61822-055-4
Library of Congress Control Number: 2017915254

To Jax

Never stop looking up...

You watch **them**.

They watch **you**.

Some are white.

Some black. Some **blue**.

All birds have **wings**.

But not all fly.

Some birds **swim**.

Others try.

Some birds **chirp**.

Others **shriek**.

And some birds sing from beak to beak.

All birds **talk**.

And so do **you**.

Come along. Let's meet a few...

Quizzical
Quail

Gliding
Wood Duck

Hungry
Hummingbird

Clingy
Woodpecker

Garrulous
Galápagos Hawks

Oyster-catching

Oystercatchers

Keen
Killdeer

Fishing
Egret

Prehistoric
Pelican

Peeking
Penguin

Glorious Goldfinch

Elevated
Eagle

**Smiling
Giggling
Laughing**
Nazca
Booby

Soulmate
Sulphur-crested Cockatoos

Flexible
Flamingos

Clapping
Cormorant

Spry
Sparrow

Hairy
Hooded
Merganser

Marching
Magellanic Penguins

Ornery
Oriole

Resting
Roadrunner

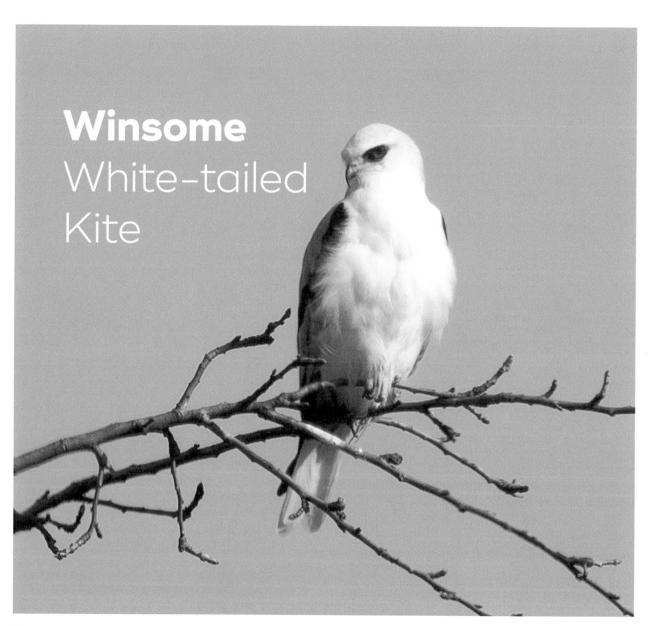

Winsome
White-tailed
Kite

Noisy
Northern
Flicker

Curious
Kingfisher

Spying Spotted Towhee

Nosy
Northern Mockingbird

Gazing
Great Blue Heron

Mysterious
Mallard

Solitary
Snowy Plover

Bright-eyed
Blue-footed
Booby

Elegant
Snowy Egret

Wading
Willet

Territorial
Turkey Vulture

Scouting
Scrub Jay

Alert
American
Robin

Gaggle of Gulls

Amiable
American Coot

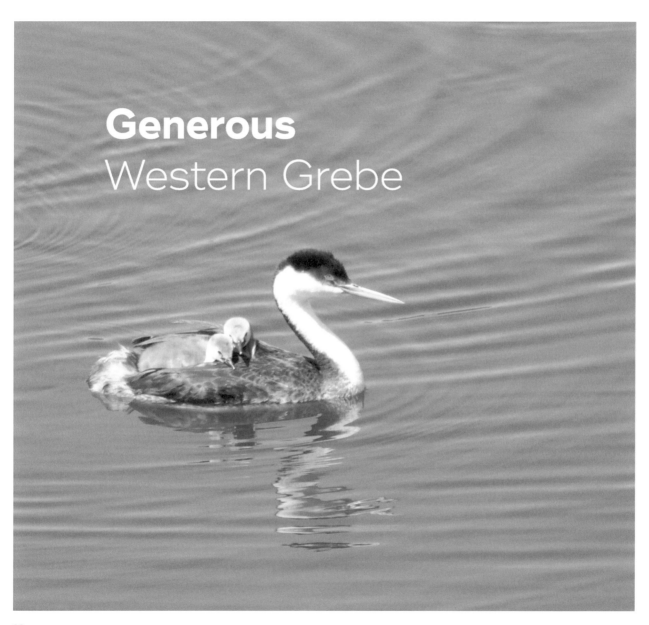

Generous
Western Grebe

Wandering Whimbrel

Friendly
Finch

Timid
Towhee

Attentive
Terns

Singing
Blackbird

Flustered Gnatcatcher

Persistent
Gentoo Penguins

Hovering
Hawk

Grounded
Golden–crowned
Sparrow

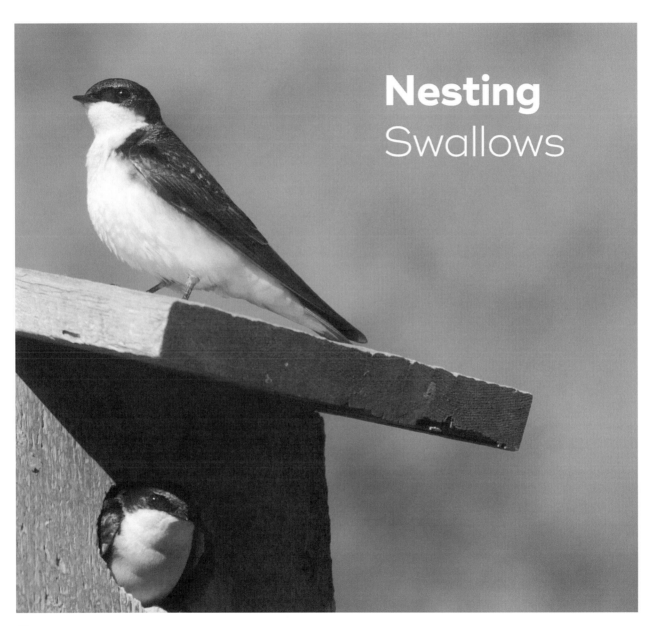

Nesting Swallows

Snacking
Starling

Racing
Red-tailed
Hawk

About the Photograher

John Yunker is an author and photographer of all things wild. (He himself comes from the wilder side of the animal kingdom.) John writes plays, short stories, and novels, and while he photographs all species of animals, his favorite subjects are those with feathers. Visit him at www.johnyunker.com.

About the Publisher

Ashland Creek Press is an independent, vegan-owned publisher of ecofiction, which includes books in all genres about animals, the environment, and the planet we all call home. We are passionate about books that foster an appreciation for worlds outside our own, for nature and the animal kingdom, and for the ways in which we all connect. To learn more, visit us at www.AshlandCreekPress.com.

CPSIA information can be obtained
at www.ICGtesting.com
Printed in the USA
LVRC02n1043251017
553478LV00002B/2

9 781618 220554